BEACH HUTS AND BATHING MACHINES

Kathryn Ferry

SHIRE PUBLICATIONS

First published in Great Britain in 2009 by Shire
Publications Ltd, Midland House, West Way, Botley,
Oxford OX2 0PH, United Kingdom.
443 Park Avenue South, New York, NY 10016, USA.

E-mail: shire@shirebooks.co.uk   www.shirebooks.co.uk

A CIP catalogue record for this book is available from the
British Library.

Shire Library no. 480   •   ISBN-978 0 7478 0700 1

Kathryn Ferry has asserted her right under the Copyright,
Designs and Patents Act, 1988, to be identified as the
author of this book.

Designed by Ken Vail Graphic Design, Cambridge, UK and
typeset in Perpetua and Gill Sans.
Printed in China through Worldprint Ltd.

09 10 11 12 13   10 9 8 7 6 5 4 3 2 1

COVER IMAGE
Beach huts on the sand at Southwold, Suffolk.

TITLE PAGE IMAGE
A horse-drawn bathing machine heading for the sea at
Woolacombe, North Devon, in 1930. Wheeled changing
rooms were a feature of British seaside resorts for two
centuries.

CONTENTS PAGE IMAGE
Beach-hut names provide an opportunity for decoration as
well as creative thinking. This example comes from
Southwold in Suffolk, where almost every hut has a name.

ACKNOWLEDGEMENTS
My thanks to Tim Baber, Sue Berry, Bob Bradley and the
staff of Margate Museum, Judy Lindsay, Heather and Tony
Payne, Mr F. L. Pettman, Olive Pigney, Malcolm Taylor,
Michael Trainor, Jon Webster at Scarborough Library, and
Gary Winter. Special thanks are also due to my parents,
Michael and Vanessa Ferry, to Matthew Slocombe for his
support and patient proof reading, and to Dan and Lottie
Slocombe for joining me on so many trips to look at beach
huts.

Illustrations are acknowledged as follows:

Dr Sue Berry pages 6 (top), and 10 (bottom); North
Yorkshire County Council Libraries pages 4, and 14 (top);
Kent County Council, Margate Library, page 7 (bottom);
Margate Museum, pages 6 (bottom), and 8 (bottom);
Malcolm Taylor, page 8 (top); Dorset County Museum,
page 10 (top); Mr F. L. Pettman pages 16 (top), 28 (left),
and 30 (bottom); Broadstairs and St Peter's Council, page
24; John Hinde pages 29 (bottom), and 46 (middle); Olive
Pigney page 36; Michael Ferry, page 58 (top); page 59 (left
and right), courtesy of Bathing Beauties™, photos by
Michael Trainor, UK; page 60 courtesy of Bathing
Beauties™, photo by Quinlan Osborne.

Shire Publications is supporting the Woodland Trust, the UK's leading woodland conservation charity, by funding the dedication of trees.

CONTENTS

THE BATHING MACHINE

BEACH HUTS have become icons of the British seaside. Despite their small size and lack of basic facilities, their popularity has reached new heights at the beginning of the twenty-first century, with prices soaring into tens of thousands of pounds. Colourful, quirky buildings on the margin between land and sea, they are immensely photogenic and, in recent years, have been used by advertisers to provide a summery backdrop to the display of such design-conscious products as clothes and mobile phones. Beach huts have an undoubted aesthetic appeal. Their simple structure is easily recognisable although their designs can differ markedly from place to place. Perhaps surprisingly, this stylistic variety is something that beach huts inherited from their wheeled forebears, bathing machines.

For almost two hundred years the bathing machine was a ubiquitous feature of the seaside landscape. It was essentially a beach hut on wheels, a sort of mobile changing room pulled directly into the sea by a horse or, where the shore was too steep, by a capstan and rope. After paying the hire charge, would-be bathers waited by the shore for a machine to become free and then stepped up into the dark, dank box in which they would remove their clothes. Windows were rarely provided, so there was little light to change by, and when the machine got moving the jerks of the horse made it an even more difficult task. In the early days women paid for guides or 'dippers', who helped them into loose-fitting, sack-style bathing gowns before taking charge of the ritual act of bathing. Though men traditionally chose to bathe naked, they still disrobed in a bathing machine so as to make their entry into the water as decent as possible.

By modern standards, it is hard to see their appeal, yet the eighteenth-century invention of bathing machines solved two clear problems associated with the new fashion for sea bathing. It was the search for better health that initially led people to the coast, spurred on by the writings of medical men who promoted first cold water and then salt water as the new miracle cure. As a result, patients would not necessarily be well enough to walk across the sands and, even if they were, the second issue of how to maintain a measure

Opposite:
The earliest known image of a bathing machine, from John Settrington's 1735 view of Scarborough. The square vehicle has a side window, pyramidal roof and four small wheels. All the bathers in this engraving are naked.

5

Bathing machines were originally met in the sea by a guide or 'dipper' whose job it was to administer the prescribed number of health-giving plunges. Aquatint from *Harry and Lucy's Trip to Brighton* by Whittemore (c.1829).

Salt Water (1798) by Thomas Rowlandson depicts several women bathing naked from the same Margate machine. In the background an unwilling client is forcibly dipped by her guide. The hood was supposed to stop men ever witnessing scenes like this.

of modesty when undressing remained. The bathing machine combined a means of transporting the sick with a private place to change and leave possessions. It is no coincidence that the first known reference to an early form of this vehicle, mentioned by the diarist Nicholas Blundell at Liverpool in 1721, refers to it as 'a *Conveniency* for Bathing in the Sea'.

Nearly a century earlier, the Yorkshire town of Scarborough became the world's first seaside resort when a mineral spring was discovered below the cliffs in 1626. In truth, however, the sea did not become a profitable element of Scarborough's spa package until several decades later when Dr Robert Wittie of Hull suggested drinking it could cure gout and balance the humours. In 1701–2 another medical man, Sir John Floyer from Lichfield, published his authoritative *History of Cold Bathing*, a book whose advocacy of shocking the system with a cold-water plunge became the manual for a new craze.

By the time John Settrington drew his panoramic view of Scarborough in 1735 wealthy people were prepared to travel long distances over poor roads for

a dip in the medicinal ocean. Settrington illustrated a few of their number cavorting naked in Scarborough's South Bay, where, at the water's edge, he recorded a strange square box mounted on four small wheels and with a pyramidal roof. This is the earliest known illustration of a bathing machine.

Yet calling it a bathing 'machine' is not quite correct; people at the time did not know what to call these new vehicles. Within ten years Scarborough had quite a number of examples designed in a more recognisable rectangular shape with pitched roofs, referred to by one observer as 'Wooden Houses movable on wheels'. They could also be found at other seaside resorts. Dr Richard Russell, author of a *Dissertation on the Use of Sea-Water in Diseases of the Glands, particularly, The Scurvy, Jaundice, King's Evil, Leprosy and the Glandular Consumption* (1750–2) and the man credited with putting Brighton on the map, described the Sussex variety as 'bathing chariots'. A contemporary visitor to Margate observed 'cover'd carriages' in use at the Kent town.

Beale's hooded machine was quickly adopted at other seaside resorts, including Southend-on-Sea, seen here c.1810.

A diagram from the 1760s showing how to use Benjamin Beale's modesty hood. After waiting at the bathing room (A), bathers boarded a 'machine' (B), the canopy of which was unfurled in deep water (D).

This token could be exchanged for a dip at Lowestoft in 1795. Beneath the hood of the left-hand bathing machine is an area of diagonal hatching that represents the lattice cage unique to this Suffolk resort.

While it is impossible to be sure who had the original idea and where, we do know that the name 'bathing machine' was first used in 1753 to describe the carriage invented at Margate by Benjamin Beale. It was very specifically called a 'machine' because on to the basic covered wagon in use elsewhere Beale added a sophisticated hood or umbrella that could be unfurled in the sea using a system of lines operated at the other end by the driver. This provided an enclosed space for the bather when entering the water. The proud author of a Margate guidebook described the apparatus as follows:

The Umbrella is formed of light Canvas spread on four Hoops. The Height of each is seven Feet, and each is eight Feet at its Axis. The last Hoop falls to a horizontal Level with its Axis, from whence depends the Curtain. The Pieces which support the Hoops are about six Feet in Length; they are fastened to the Bottom of the Machine, but are extended by a small Curve, about one Foot wider than the Body of it on each Side. The Hoops move in Grooves in these Pieces. The Distance of the Axis of the first Hoop is more than two Feet from the Machine; of the rest from each other, something more than one Foot; but no greater Exactness is required in these Proportions, as scarce any two of them are built alike.

Bathing machines in Margate harbour, drawn by T. Smith in 1810. Cabins were mounted high above the wheels, so the hood was finished with a skirt that met the water.

Because of this new mechanism, bathers could undergo the prescribed number of medicinal dunkings in private. Given that few people in the mid eighteenth century could swim and their first introduction to the vast ocean was likely to be in winter at the hands of a guide paid to push their head repeatedly below the waves, privacy was a clear benefit. Beale's invention was quickly taken up and Margate's popularity increased as a result of his innovation. As a competitor for the lucrative London tourist trade, Brighton pointedly refused to adopt the hood but at both resorts the once stagnant economies were revitalised by sea bathing.

A naked King George III is welcomed into the waves by a band of musicians. Within days of his first dip at Weymouth this souvenir engraving by John Nixon could be bought on the streets of London.

It was the promise of a new source of income that led other coastal towns to set themselves up as sea-bathing places. In this new venture the provision of bathing machines was a prerequisite. Local entrepreneurs often took the initiative, as at Lowestoft, which got its first bathing machine in 1769, provided by the landlord of the Crown Inn. It proved so popular with members of the Suffolk gentry that five more were soon acquired. These had hoods according to the Margate model but late-eighteenth-century illustrations also show a unique addition: attached below the hood was a sort of low lattice cage that provided a fence around the bathing area.

Like so many fashions, sea bathing began as an exclusive pursuit of the moneyed classes; only they could afford to spend extended periods away from home. Hiring a bathing machine was an expensive activity, which consequently became a status symbol. Ralph Allen, a key figure in the development of Georgian Bath, kept his own machine at Weymouth, where he also had a holiday home. Influential patrons like Allen were a great boon to any up-and-coming seaside resort but Weymouth was also lucky enough to be favoured by the Duke of Gloucester, and then, in 1789, by his elder brother, King George III, who was suffering from the first bout of a recurring illness. His Majesty's doctors recommended a series of dips on the Dorset coast. The townspeople showed their delight by providing a band to serenade King George on his first excursion into the sea, where, stepping naked from an octagonal bathing machine, he was met by female attendants whose bonnets were decorated with the motto 'God save the King'.

The King's machine was larger than normal and on the pyramidal roof, above its landward door, was fixed the royal coat of arms. A visitor of 1852 noted that it had been preserved with the addition of an inscription, which read: 'The machine of the great and good King George III, the friend of the poor, the patron of Weymouth'. Still in regular use until 1914, the royal

The octagonal machine reputedly used by George III, with the royal crest above its door, was still in use until the First World War. Other octagonal machines can be seen in the background of this Edwardian photograph.

In late-eighteenth-century Brighton the process of bathing could be rather disorderly, with several people typically chasing the same machine. *Bathing Machines* by Thomas Rowlandson from *An Excursion to Brighthelmstone* by H. Wigstead and T. Rowlandson, 1790.

machine then served as a garden summerhouse before its eventual donation to Weymouth Museum in 1971.

The Prince Regent (later King George IV) eschewed Weymouth and favoured Brighton as his seaside resort of choice. It is a shame that, having created such an exotic confection as the Royal Pavilion, he did not also commission a matching bathing machine complete with onion domes and Chinese wallpaper. He was certainly a regular bather under the supervision of Martha Gunn, the most famous 'dipper' in history, and swimming instructor John 'Smoaker' Miles. Both proved such faithful servants that their portraits feature among the Royal Collection.

Hoods were still in use on Ramsgate beach in 1863. Deck chairs had yet to be invented, so local people hired out their household seats to tourists.

By the time Queen Victoria came to the throne in 1837 Brighton was a busy and popular resort with a reputation for hedonism that owed much to George IV's love of parties and pleasure. The young Queen disliked the architecture of her uncle's Pavilion and found Brighton people 'very indiscreet and troublesome', so, with her German husband, she chose a holiday retreat on the Isle of Wight instead. It was in the grounds of Osborne House in July 1847 that she took her first ever dip in the sea from a specially designed bathing machine. This luxurious vehicle was hand-crafted by a Portsmouth coachbuilder. Under its pitched roof the machine measured 12 feet by 7 feet. Inside there were dressing rooms and a plumbed-in water closet. The door and window handles were made of silver and a deep canopy shaded the steps leading into the sea.

With or without the silver handles, for most of the population of early-nineteenth-century Britain hiring a bathing machine remained an infrequent, if not impossible luxury. In the first place they needed the time and money to get to the coast. But the coming of steam power meant huge and rapid change, making journeys to the seaside both quicker and cheaper. As the railways spread across the country, more and more people were able to enjoy a seaside holiday or, at the very least, a day excursion. In the summer of 1852 one journalist remarked on how much city dwellers yearned to escape: 'People hear the surf in the rumble of the omnibuses, and instinctively sniff for the smell of sea-weed in the hot choky vapours of the narrow street; bathing machines become gorgeous dreams of expectancy.' The increase in visitor numbers was phenomenal. To take just one example, in 1837 around 50,000 passengers travelled to Brighton by stage-coach during the course of the year: in 1850 the railway carried 73,000 in a single week. Pleasure had superseded health as the main reason to travel to the coast and with this new influx of people the beaches were getting crowded.

When at the Seaside
Don't forget the
number of
your machine!

VICTORIAN VARIATIONS

B Y 1800 bathing machines had become *the* accessory to sea bathing – so much so that for the rest of the nineteenth century it was considered improper to enter the sea without one. This was a social nicety encouraged by resort authorities constantly trying to regulate the behaviour of visitors who wanted to let their hair down at the seaside. Working-class trippers who had one day a year to take the coast-bound train were understandably keen to feel the salty waves on their skin but better-off visitors afraid of losing their peace and exclusivity took the moral high ground by lobbying for beach regulations. Because of this pressure, by the 1860s most seaside resorts had enacted by-laws to segregate male and female bathing areas. In practice, this draconian separation proved less successful than middle-class moralists would have liked. The distance between ladies' and gentlemen's machines did not stop voyeurism on either side and, since vehicles were supposed to move with the tide, there could often be confusion when trying to return to one's machine, a theme well tested by cartoonists of the period.

Bathing machines were not invented by prudish Victorians, but the mid to late nineteenth century was certainly their heyday. Their use was made compulsory on most main resort beaches, which meant that excursionists unable to afford the fee had to make do with a paddle in the shallows. Proprietors tended to be private individuals for whom the seasonal hire of bathing machines supplemented other full-time work as boatmen, fishermen, boarding-house keepers, publicans or shopkeepers. Even the smallest resorts usually had a few machines and since bathing was a core attraction the standard of accommodation was important: improvements were patented and owners created distinctive designs for their locality.

At Scarborough a local undertaker named T. W. Crosby introduced his 'Patent Safety Bathing Machine' in about 1853. This ingenious contraption aimed to provide a truly private bathing experience by letting sea water into the machine itself. From a raised dressing room at the landward end bathers could step down into a pool of water let in through low-level louvres in the door and floor. Although Crosby's machine seems to have been built, it did

Opposite:
Bathing grounds for men and women were supposed to be separate but this did not always work in practice. Mistaking your machine could be quite uncomfortable, as this blushing fellow found out!

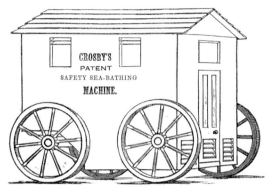 

not prove a success. Birmingham resident Hugo Westman was less innovative in his patented improvements, but his machine, with its angled steps, three upper side panels and low arched roof designed to provide 'the required height while limiting the area exposed to the wind', was adopted in Brighton, where it appeared in Edwardian postcard views.

Although Westman's patent made reference to interior furnishings, these do not seem to have been radically different to well-established provision. Machines usually featured a bench to sit on, a mirror and high-level hooks or pegs for hanging dry clothes and hats. Westman suggested adding a dressing table but one Devon proprietor's boast of carpeted bathing machines was probably a home comfort too far!

Coastal geography combined with local manufacturing abilities meant that there was never a standard bathing-machine design, and the introduction

Brighton machines built to the patented specifications of Hugo Westman. For better wind resistance, the roof was 'raised and slightly arched in the middle and lower at each side'.

of picture postcards in the mid 1890s enables us to get a sense of the wide variety in use around the coast. The basic functional necessity of a machine that was heavy enough to stand firm in the waves and remain unmoved, despite a constant slap of water against the underside of the floor, produced different solutions in different places. To allow wave room, cabins in Kent were raised on stilts mounted on the axle beds, whereas in Sussex wheels were made with a much larger diameter. Wheel size also seems to have been determined by the type of beach and whether the machine had to travel across fine soft sand, firm hard sand or shingle. To counteract the effect of a sloping shore, front wheels would often be bigger than those at the rear, a disparity that could look very strange when the machines were parked on the flat. In a few places, such as Jersey and Ilfracombe, Devon, machines travelled only as far as the water's edge and so their wheels were much smaller and the floors of their changing rooms were much closer to the ground.

I wouldn't leave my little woooden hut for you.

Kent resorts had a well-established precedent in Benjamin Beale's Margate machine but by the late nineteenth century this design, with its high-set cabin, had been adapted and enlarged. With its side walls jettied out over the wheels, each machine was divided into two cubicles, the modesty hood replaced by triangular wooden screens. At bathing time a more efficient system was also introduced, with rows of machines arranged in seaborne terraces. To save the time wasted in pulling

The typical interior features of a bathing machine were bench, mirror and clothes hooks. Towels and bathing costumes were often hired with the machine.

Bathing at Jersey.

As the sands were flat on this Jersey beach, machines could be rolled along on small wooden wheels. Diamond-shaped holes were cut in the gables for ventilation.

15

'A Water Frolic' at Cliftonville near Margate. These double machines were built and run by the Pettman family. To save time, they would be lined up in the sea with parties of bathers ferried out by horse and cart.

each vehicle back and forth, bathers were ferried out by horse and cart, picked up from a wheeled staging on the beach at Margate, or from a purpose-built waiting platform at neighbouring Cliftonville. It was at Cliftonville that the Pettman family operated their successful bathing establishment, offering 'fully one hundred most comfortable and thoroughly ventilated bathing machines, all constructed on Mr Pettman's premises and designed according to the latest modern principles'. A souvenir brochure published by Pettman stated that he also built these updated machines for nearby resorts.

At high tide the rows of Cliftonville machines could be accessed via a purpose-built platform.

The sentry-box style of machine was adopted right along the Sussex coast. Large wheels were a distinctive feature and the bather standing in the left foreground at Bognor Regis helps give a sense of their impressive scale.

Originally part of the Hounsom family fleet, this Eastbourne machine was rescued from an allotment and meticulously restored by Julian Martyr of the Langham Hotel. The colour scheme was identified from analysis of paint scrapings.

Sussex machines derived their shape from the eighteenth-century 'bathing chariots' of Brighton. This sentry-box style, described by one critic in 1871 as resembling 'an overgrown dog kennel', could be seen on beaches from Hastings to Bognor Regis. Made from panels of vertical tongue and groove, the cabin was carried between pairs of impressively large wheels, 60 inches in diameter, with fourteen spokes and a $4\frac{1}{2}$ - inch rim banded with iron. Paint scrapings taken from a restored Eastbourne machine show that they were also highly colourful; the Hounsom family's fleet was painted with stripes of bright red and yellow. With its clear nautical associations, blue and white was another popular colour scheme. Mr W. J. Flint of Bexhill chose it for his machines and mentioned the fact when advertising his services. This was not simply for aesthetic reasons; it also made good business sense when there was more than one company offering machines on the same strip of sand. For example, in Brighton at the beginning of the 1870s there were 254 licensed public bathing machines managed by twenty different proprietors. Victorian and Edwardian photographs may show us a world in black and white but we should imagine bathing machines as a vibrant, if not gaudy, element of the seaside landscape.

He. "What will you do love when I am going"
She. Try Beecham's Pills.

Advertisement for Beecham's Pills from the early 1890s. Beecham's was one of several companies that used the sides of bathing machines as mobile hoardings.

If modern beach huts have inherited the right to be bright from their wheeled ancestors, the idea that they can help market unrelated products was also first tested by the Victorians. Bathing machines featured in advertisements for Bovril and Beecham's Pills but they were also turned into mobile hoardings on the beach. So many potential consumers were now spending time at the seaside that this was a shrewd way of reaching a captive audience. Brand names such as Pears and Sunlight soap, Singer sewing machines and Beecham's Pills could be seen painted on to the sides of bathing machines up and down the coast.

As in Kent and Sussex, a regional type appeared also on the East Anglian coast from Felixstowe to Clacton. Here horizontal timber planks were strengthened by an exposed frame that could appear as decorative arcading. A similar method of construction was used for wooden threshing machines, suggesting an overlap of techniques and probably also labour, from the agricultural hinterland.

In Northumberland the bathing machines at Tynemouth and Whitley Bay had a unique maritime quality that came from employing construction methods usually applied to boatbuilding. The clinker-built cabins were made

West Beach and Jetty, Clacton-on-Sea.

Bathing machines at Clacton, showing the decorative arcading peculiar to this part of Essex and Suffolk. At the shore end bathers walked along the attached gangplank, which trailed behind the machine on a small pair of skid wheels.

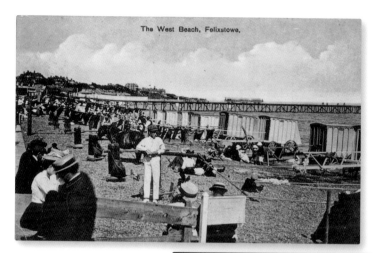

The West Beach, Felixstowe.

At Felixstowe machines were moved using capstans and rope. Note how the lines of hired bathing costumes were strung across the beach to dry.

The resemblance between these Northumberland machines and the shape of an upturned boat is more than coincidental. At Whitley Bay and Tynemouth the same construction techniques were used for both.

South Sands, Tenby

Machines at Tenby, Pembrokeshire, had shallow arched roofs and big iron wheels. They varied in colour but the walls of most carried advertisements for Beecham's Pills.

The family-sized machines at Gorleston in Norfolk looked like Romany caravans. There were also bell tents on the beach, and in the foreground towels have been laid out to dry.

This photograph of c.1895 shows the kiosk-style machines introduced to the Devon resort of Paignton some twenty years earlier. They were distinguished by an unusual peaked roof, topped with a decorative finial.

The wheeled saloons at Weymouth provided multiple changing rooms with direct sea access. In this Edwardian photograph, three men return to the beach along a flimsy-looking walkway.

of horizontal planks bent into shape between the arched door openings at either end, giving the impression of a boat's hull stretched and upturned.

Elsewhere around the coast other unusual designs eschewed the basic form of a box with a pitched roof. The shallow-arched barrel roof was one popular alternative. At Gorleston, in Norfolk, Mr Capps and his sons used this shape to especially good effect on their double-width family machines. These had two doors on the landward side leading into a vestibule with a single door opening on to the sea. The roof extended beyond the front and rear of the machine, held up on decorative curved brackets, creating a design reminiscent of Romany caravans.

The most individual roof shape was to be found on the machines in use at Glentworth Bay, Weston-super-Mare, Somerset, from the 1850s. Some twenty years later this design found its way to Paignton and Oddicombe in south Devon. Here the panelled rectangular cabins were held fast to the chassis by four diagonal brackets, the halted upward thrust of which was terminated more gracefully by a pyramidal, tent-like roof. Oriental flourishes could often be found in seaside architecture, particularly on piers, but this theme had little impact on bathing machine design. Only these wheeled kiosks from the West Country showed any hint of exoticism. A little further east, at Budleigh Salterton, machines with similar panelled sides were introduced in the 1880s. Made of oak, they were painted blue and white. What made them unusual was their hexagonal shape.

From 1889 Walter Fagg's patent bathing carriages ran on tramlines across Folkestone beach. Each carriage could supply the same accommodation as fifteen traditional machines.

Two Dutch ladies pose next to the driver's seat of a bathing machine at Scheveningen. The double roof feature was probably intended to improve ventilation inside the machine.

The only other place with polygonal bathing machines was Weymouth, where King George III's machine inspired a fleet of octagonal changing rooms, in use alongside more conventional-looking examples until about 1919. A guidebook writer at the end of the nineteenth century remarked that 'the town authorities and private enterprise have provided an abundance of machines. They are more roomy than is usually the case, and what is more important, are much better ventilated.' In 1900 the charge, including costume and towel, was 6d, or 4d per person for two sharing. A cheaper option was to use one of the large bathing saloons unique to Weymouth, which cost just 2d per person. There were four saloons, two for men and two for women, supposedly positioned at a modest distance from each other. Essentially just elongated bathing machines, these saloons could accommodate fifty-two people in separate cabins and were accessed by a rickety-looking series of raised planks.

The idea of multiple changing rooms in a single vehicle reached its apogee at Folkestone, Kent, where Walter David Fagg, local councillor and manager of the Folkestone Bathing Establishment Company, patented and built his 'Safety Bathing Carriage' to run on tramlines into the sea. Made up of twenty-nine cabins opening on to a central corridor, the carriage was mounted on an iron frame fitted with wheels of differing sizes, designed to keep the floor horizontal whatever the state of tide. At the sea end there was a 'safety crate', a sort of submerged cage, for the benefit of non-swimmers. Fagg's carriage enjoyed its first season in 1889 and appears to have kept running until about 1912. According to one satisfied customer from London, it was the 'finest invention of the Victorian era', quite a claim for a period of such technological progress!

Bathing machines were adopted throughout the British Isles; they were also exported around the world. Instances of their use can be found in the United States, Australia and New Zealand, albeit with less success than in northern Europe. Many French resorts had machines and there was a particularly large fleet at Boulogne, perhaps because it was so popular with, and easily accessible to, British tourists. There, the distinctive panelled design

99   BOULOGNE-SUR-MER. — L'Heure du Bain. — Bathing-time. — LL.

The French Channel resort of Boulogne had a large fleet of bathing machines. Unlike most British examples, they had only one door set into a porch at the seaward end. The other end was often rounded.

was rounded at one end, with the seaward-facing door set back inside a kind of porch. At Scheveningen in the Netherlands, the coastal resort for The Hague, machines were available to hire in two sizes, large or small. In Belgium, too, beaches were cluttered with bathing machines, none more so than at King Leopold's royal resort of Ostend. This was where machines reached their definitive decorative expression. Introduced at the end of the nineteenth century, the *machine de luxe* proclaimed its luxury status in its fine construction and paintwork, its ornate roof details and its windows engraved with scenes of the surrounding area. For all the regional ingenuity of British designs, it was the Belgians who built the ultimate bathing machine.

Ostende. — Cabine de luxe.   N. 88.

Ostend, in Belgium, was the only place to develop 'luxury' bathing machines. The hire price was three times that of an ordinary machine. Note how the attendant sitting on horseback is wearing the same stripes as his machine.

23

PRIVATE TENTS

FOR HIRE ON BROADSTAIRS SANDS AT THE MAIN BAY, LOUISA BAY AND DUMPTON BAY

Tents are available for weekly hirings (long or short periods) commencing on Saturday, the 30th March, 1929, continuing throughout the Season, which will terminate on Friday, 25th October, 1929.   Early bookings are desirable.

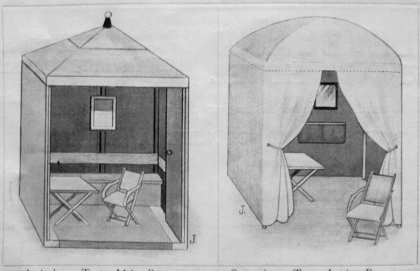

A lock-up Tent. Main Bay type.   Open front Tent. Louisa Bay type.

All Tents offered for hire are of modern construction, and are situated in excellent positions on the sands with direct access to the sea. Tents are furnished with wooden floor, locker, table, chair and mirror, and other modern conveniences.

MODERATE INCLUSIVE WEEKLY CHARGES

Tents may now be booked for the ensuing season. Full particulars and scale of charges may be obtained on application to the :—

Entertainments Manager, Broadstairs and St. Peter's Urban District Council, Pierremont Hall, Broadstairs.

Personal enquiries should be made at the Enquiry and Booking Office, base of Albion Steps (Main Bay Sands), where a plan of sites may be inspected. Office open daily all the year round.

TENTS, BUNGALOWS AND BATHING STATIONS

A T the end of the nineteenth century bathing machines were still very much a part of the seaside scene but things were beginning to change. During the Edwardian and inter-war periods new structures appeared on the beach which gradually took over from the old wheeled variety.

In 1895 a national newspaper campaign began with the aim of reintroducing 'mixed' bathing. People with influence were now more embarrassed by what they saw as the outmoded separation of men and women than they were by the idea of bathing with members of the opposite sex. There had been complaints before, making unfavourable comparison between British customs and those on the Continent, particularly France, where greater freedom prevailed. These complaints gained weight as resorts came to realise that they were losing business to their foreign rivals. The economic argument had always been stronger than the moral one and it was at the resorts most dependent on wealthy tourists that mixed bathing was first officially reintroduced, in places such as Llandudno, Paignton, Cromer and Dawlish. It was partly because men affirmed the right to bathe naked throughout the nineteenth century that this situation had taken so long to come about, but provided men and women were properly clothed they were now free to share the same stretch of water. Countrywide, change happened gradually and the continuing novelty of mixed bathing was reflected in comic postcards from the turn of the century. Nonetheless, public opinion had shifted and, though bathing machines clung on through the 1930s, their days were numbered.

The first step towards modern beach huts was the introduction of a static, semi-permanent type of changing room. British tourists who had crossed the Channel praised the use of tents at resorts such as Dieppe, which had never had bathing machines because of its steeply sloping shore. Although other European resorts, in France, Belgium, the Netherlands and Spain, did have wheeled changing rooms, the idea of tent bathing, adopted in Britain at the same time as mixed bathing, took on an air of Continental sophistication.

Whereas bathing machines were hired per bathe, usually for about half an hour, tents could be taken by the day, week or season. Pitches were also

Opposite:
An advertisement from the 1929 guide to Broadstairs, showing the two types of beach tent available for hire.

25

An imagined view of mixed bathing at Blackpool. The artist of this jolly scene has given each couple one fat and one thin partner!

Margate was a popular resort with trippers but to either side of the town were the more refined beaches of Cliftonville and Westbrook. The variety of tents on the sand at Westbrook suggests they were pitched by private individuals.

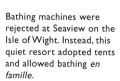

Bathing machines were rejected at Seaview on the Isle of Wight. Instead, this quiet resort adopted tents and allowed bathing *en famille*.

set aside for people to erect their own tents bought from local retailers or department stores. For the first time families were able to establish a proper beach base. Temporary tent villages sprang up on the sands of smart Edwardian resorts, attracting tourists who sought peaceful relaxation rather than the noisy pleasures of more populist seaside towns. To begin with, the cost of this convenience ruled out the working class.

The earliest British use of beach tents has gone unrecorded but makeshift, tent-like shelters were certainly used on remote beaches during the Victorian period. Round bell-tents, of the type used in army camps, can be seen in seaside photographs from the late nineteenth century. By the early 1900s they came in many different shapes and sizes, square or round, with pointed or flat roofs and plain white canvas or brightly striped sides. One pioneering resort was the village of Seaview on the Isle of Wight, where the colourful line of tents looked particularly picturesque against a backdrop of green trees. A guidebook writer of 1897 praised the liberal approach to bathing at Seaview: 'whoever is responsible for the substitution of bathing tents for the hideous machines that disfigure most sea-side places, deserves the gratitude of the community.'

More usually, tents were available alongside traditional bathing machines, so as to cater for all preferences. The key difference between the two modes of bathing was proximity to the sea; changing in a machine generally allowed direct access to the water while changing in a tent meant walking across the beach to get there. Being seen in one's bathing costume was still considered quite daring, and not everyone was ready to show off their physique. One solution was to don a cloak in the French fashion; another was to put the tents on wheels. As early as 1871, there were twenty of these useful hybrids

White tents with small wooden wheels line up along the water's edge at Swanage in Dorset. These were intermediate between bathing machines and static tents.

Above:
A family outside their own tent at Cliftonville. For a small charge Mr Pettman would store private tents when not in use.

Above right:
This family holidayed at Broadstairs for several years during the 1920s and always hired a tent. The young girl in the foreground has temporarily abandoned her bucket and spade while her parents have tea.

at Littlehampton in Sussex. Provided by the corporation, they measured 6 feet square, with solid wooden floors. Because of their wheels, these tents could be pushed over the shingle on to hard sand, saving the bather's feet the discomfort of walking. Similar wheeled tents later appeared at the Dorset resorts of Swanage and Lyme Regis, while at Dawlish in Devon they ran along a purpose-built track.

Beach tents continued to be popular in the twentieth century and a modern version can still be seen today. These simple lightweight structures proved a useful way of meeting seasonal demand. To prolong their life, hired tents were often given a wooden frame and the canvas walls could be weatherproofed with a coat of whitewash. In the 1920s, holidaymakers at Broadstairs in Kent could hire two different types of tent from the council; one had an open fabric front, and on the other canvas was stretched across a timber frame to make lockable doors. Both came with a wooden floor, locker, table, chair and mirror. Their descendants are still in use. At Weymouth distinctive tent skeletons have been part of the beach scene since the 1920s. The wooden frame stays on the shore all summer, with its canvas wall panels stored in a locker at the back.

In functional terms there was clearly a lot of overlap between tents and beach huts, something that is discussed in the next chapter. The range of

Wooden tent skeletons on Weymouth beach. Integral lockers provide storage for the canvas wall panels that can be put up when needed.

names given to seaside changing rooms can be very confusing but tents did begin as a distinctive type of structure, as did bathing 'bungalows'.

These days the word 'bungalow' speaks of mass housing, a form of single-storey dwelling widespread in Britain's towns and cities. Although there are few people today who would attach much romance to the name, this was not the case for the Edwardians. Bungalows originated in India, and the first western examples were built from the 1870s on the cliff tops of Birchington

Beach tents remained popular after the Second World War. This 1960s view of Porthminster Beach, St Ives, makes Cornwall look almost tropical with its bright canvas tents and palm tree.

The basic Edwardian design of Bournemouth's beach huts has changed very little over the years.

The price list for 'Pettman's Unrivalled Sea Bathing' shows the range of options available in the early 1900s. Tent hire specifically came under the heading of 'Family Bathing'.

and Westgate-on-Sea in Kent. They were designed as upper-middle-class seaside homes – isolated escapes within easy reach of London. Among the early occupants were artistic, Bohemian types, whose link to the word 'bungalow' lent it glamorous, even racy connotations. The name was also adopted to describe the converted railway carriages and wooden holiday shacks that began to appear around the coast from the 1890s, built by people seeking an inexpensive and individual place to stay by the sea.

When the new Undercliff Drive was created at up-and-coming Bournemouth in 1908, it featured a line of day huts that were the first municipally built bungalows, so called to capitalise on the name's fashionable associations. At 10 feet square, they provided families with 'a storeroom for books, spades, pails and all the impedimenta of seaside life and facilities for simple meals'. In front of each glazed front door was an individual sitting area sheltered by the roof's overhang and, in the early days, shaded by a canvas awning.

Pettman's Unrivalled Sea Bathing.

CHARGES.

At the Bathing Station, NEWGATE CUTTING
(Near Queen's Hotel).

The Staircase opposite the OVAL BANDSTAND.

Use of Bathing Machine or Pavilion, **6d.** each person, or book of 12 Tickets		**5/-**
Use of Costume	... ...	**2d.**
Two Towels or one large one	... ...	**1d.**

Children bathing from Cabin, **2d.** each.

TENT & PAVILION BATHING STATION, WALPOLE BAY.
Entrance by the New Steps from Queen's Promenade.

Bathing from Tents ... ... **4d.** each person

FOR FAMILY BATHING.

Hire of Tent... .. ... from **1/6** per day or **8/-** per week
Special Bathing Pavilion (including fresh water shower and hot water foot bath)
4d. each person

At Cliftonville the Pettmans also realised the potency of the name and turned some of their bathing machines into what they liked to call 'Bungalow Town'.

The next innovation occurred at Scarborough's North Bay. As at Bournemouth, the sandy top of the beach was being replaced by a new asphalt promenade. To prettify a functional walkway and improve visitor facilities, the Borough Surveyor, Harry W. Smith, designed a row of bungalows. In contrast to the detached Bournemouth variety, the first Scarborough bungalows of 1910 were built as a terrace. Each of the twelve rooms measured about 7 feet 6 inches square and had a 4 foot 6 inch open veranda in front. The beach inspector was given the central thirteenth room, which was equipped with gas, as well as hot and cold water, so that tenants could make tea. From the outset these buildings were designed to be an

Bathing bungalows were introduced by Bournemouth Corporation in 1908. They were permanent structures on the promenade but did not replace the machines, which continued to operate on the beach.

In 1910 rows of terraced bungalows appeared in Scarborough's North Bay. They were built above the promenade so that parents could keep a watchful eye as their children played on the sand.

The first bungalows at Scarborough's South Bay were built on a slight curve, with greater attention to design detail, seen here in the veranda posts. In the middle distance is Scarborough Spa and, in the background, the Grand Hotel.

Classical styles of architecture were often too formal for the beach but Sandbanks Pavilion in Dorset was a notable exception. Here the day huts were built behind a Doric colonnade.

attractive addition to the seafront and their style was overtly residential, with the timber-framed gables and multi-paned windows that were typical of Edwardian domestic architecture.

So successful did these Scarborough shelters prove that during the winter of 1911–12 a second line of thirteen was constructed, along with four semi-detached ones. At the same time, the town's traditionally more up-market South Bay was also provided with twenty bungalows of its own. By the late 1920s Scarborough's two bays had 145 bungalows between them.

Following this precedent, the block form was used in two ways during the inter-war period: first, to provide day huts on the Scarborough model,

The upper storey of this Cromer hut block has a projecting central bay and curved ends. The windows with oblong panes are typical of 1930s design. On the cliff above is a contemporary shelter with flat circular roof.

and second, to take over the role of bathing machines by offering short-hire changing cubicles.

The design of these buildings usually fell within the remit of the borough surveyor, so outside architectural firms were rarely involved. Mock Tudor timber framing was popular on hut blocks around Britain, some of which survive at places such as Weymouth, Clacton and Cromer. Elsewhere, the influence of international stylistic developments can be seen. The Pavilion (1928) at Sandbanks, near Poole, was designed by E. J. Goodacre in the sort of *Beaux-arts* classicism also employed in contemporary lido design. A shallow dome marked the mid-point of this angular crescent, and day huts were set

The West Marina Bathing Station, built in 1934 at St Leonards-on-Sea, Sussex, was almost industrial in scale. Despite a local campaign to save and restore it, this modernist hut block was demolished in 2006.

back behind a Doric colonnade. At Saltburn, Yorkshire, two blocks built into the cliff were given a rather incongruous touch of the Spanish hacienda style. Cromer's double-decker block had curved ends and flat roofs while Sidney Little, the 'Concrete King', gave St Leonards-on-Sea near Hastings the starkly modern West Marina Bathing Station. Every one of the ninety huts, spread over two levels, had its own electricity and water supply; there were built-in garages at the rear and the flat roof doubled as a sun deck.

If the curative powers of sea water had first drawn people to the seaside during the eighteenth century, in the 1920s and 1930s they came to bathe in the sun. This newest craze had a major impact on beach habits since concerns about covering the body were rapidly swept away in an attempt to expose as much flesh as possible to the health-giving solar rays.

Despite these new freedoms, the idea that swimmers should pay for a place to change into their costumes was deeply entrenched and persisted even as the bathing machine declined. Bathing stations had begun as a way of designating specific areas of the beach for bathing, usually the places where machines could be hired. During the inter-war years the term was used to describe physical structures built in these locations to provide changing cubicles and usually some type of refreshment room. To maximise space, these buildings were often of two storeys, as at Lowestoft's Victoria Bathing Station, or the vast double-decker structure with rooftop sun deck that has been a feature of Viking Bay, Broadstairs, since 1935. Although there is no evidence of outside influence, this kind of provision had long been the norm in the United States, where long rows of changing rooms under the same roof were known as 'bath-houses'.

At Broadstairs the huge concrete bathing station fills almost the entire width of Viking Bay. The flat roof was designed as a sun terrace.

The central 'refreshment buffet' and end pavilions at Lowestoft's Victoria Bathing Station give interest to an otherwise simple structure. Its horizontal form contrasts with the vertical emphasis of Victorian hotels on the cliff top.

Nowadays the bathing stations that survive have been turned into day huts. Local councils tried to stop the practice of 'mackintosh bathing' when it first began to appear in the 1920s but this was not a fight they could win. People put on their bathing costumes in the privacy of their hotel rooms, then wore a mackintosh over the top to walk to the beach. At first, resorts charged for the privilege of *not* hiring their changing rooms but after the Second World War things moved on, with the result that getting undressed on the beach became not only acceptable but normal. The concept of paying for access to the sea, which had begun with the invention of the bathing machine, was finally consigned to the past.

The metal railings at Broadstairs feature a 1930s wave design. The wooden huts in front are descended from the tents on page 24.

35

BEACH HUTS: PAST

WHEN looking back at old guidebooks, it can be hard to tell the difference between a bungalow, a beach hut and a chalet. When writers referred to 'bathing boxes' and 'cabins', were they talking about the same thing? It seems to have been a question of time and place as much as design and function, all of which makes it difficult to track down the earliest beach huts. There is a good chance, however, that Felixstowe in Suffolk can claim this honour because a row of small wooden buildings with pitched roofs was photographed beside the beach there as early as 1895. Confusingly, they were called 'tents', a description that had to be clarified for visitors. A guidebook of 1919 explained that these 'tents' were 'not tents at all but wooden structures... generally used in place of bathing machines'. Not only were they convenient for bathers, but they could also 'serve as snug and pleasant rooms where one could work, read, or dream in the shade, close to the sea'. It is a list of activities and non-activities that will be familiar to most twenty-first-century hut users!

Like Felixstowe, Bexhill-on-Sea, Sussex, flourished in the late Victorian and Edwardian years by catering for wealthy tourists. Below its promenade was a 'long file of tents and gaily coloured cabins', the latter of the wooden, pitched-roof variety. In the same way that Bournemouth deliberately chose to use the word 'bungalow', these exclusive resorts seem to have considered the idea of beach 'huts' rather too downmarket for their clientele. Irrespective of the nomenclature, these diminutive buildings shared the common purpose of providing a 'home from home'.

Their design was simple but not necessarily uniform. Whereas Bournemouth's bungalows were erected by the corporation, early huts at Felixstowe and Bexhill tended to be in mixed ownership. Most hotels and boarding houses had them for the use of guests, a tradition that continued around Britain at least into the 1960s. The 'important' houses in Felixstowe, probably summer residences owned or rented by the gentry, also had their own private beach huts. Meanwhile, at Folkestone, wealthy visitors staying in luxury hotels along The Leas could make use of architecturally innovative

Opposite:
This hut at Wells-next-the-Sea in Norfolk was built c.1924 for the Emerson family. It was made in sections by the local carpenter and coffin-maker, then taken to the beach on a high tide to be put together. In 1984 Herbert Emerson, the youngest son pictured here, sold 'Prongs' – named after a Bombay lighthouse – to Olive Pigney (see page 52).

37

These beach huts of the 1890s, at Felixstowe in Suffolk, were probably the first in Britain. They were a variety of shapes, sizes and colours because they were erected by different people, for their own use and for hire to visitors.

Taking tea in an Edwardian beach hut. The clothes may have changed a lot over the past century but the way we use beach huts has not.

The Sussex resort of Bexhill-on-Sea was proud of its liberal attitude towards bathing and was one of the first places to provide wooden beach huts or 'cabins'.

Concrete was a relatively new building material in the early 1900s but was used for these beach huts at Folkestone in Kent. The row includes some huts built side on to the sea with double window openings.

huts at the base of the cliff. Built towards the end of Edward VII's reign, they were early concrete structures with walls that were, somewhat ironically, given an exterior pattern meant to look like timber framing. The interiors of these sophisticated huts have plastered walls above varnished wood panelling.

Smaller seaside places were also adopting beach huts before the First World War. These structures nestled in the dunes of Sandbanks in Dorset and Sutton-on-Sea in Lincolnshire; they hugged the base of the cliff at Frinton-on-Sea in Essex and enjoyed the shade of the pinewoods at Wells-next-the-Sea in Norfolk. Ownership of the foreshore was rarely questioned; local people simply made use of the empty sand. This colonisation included bungalow communities of basic, often self-built holiday homes that were a cheap and deliberately independent holiday alternative. Some grew autonomously like

Early beach huts often appeared before the creation of a formal promenade. At Sutton-on-Sea in Lincolnshire some were built on wooden platforms but others simply sat in the sand dunes.

Shoreham to the west of Brighton, but others such as Peacehaven in the opposite direction and later Jaywick in Essex began as money-making speculations. These developments gathered momentum in the 1920s, the same decade that day huts also became common around the coast.

The key attraction has not changed since the 1920s. Old guidebooks liked to sum it up in the notion of a seaside 'home from home' and these little huts have always provided a much-valued family base. Away from their hotels or boarding houses, holidaymakers could temporarily claim a little piece of the seafront and relax in their own space. Parents and children could amuse themselves but the hut was always there to come back to. For children who grew up by the sea, the beach hut could be just as important; it was the background to summer days, a playhouse by the ocean.

Remarking on the popularity of huts at Bexhill, a guidebook of 1901 noted that 'many people pass practically the whole of their day on the beach. By means of a spirit kettle and a few cups the high function of afternoon tea may be celebrated with the minimum of inconvenience, and some enthusiasts even go to the length of collecting the material for wood fires and frying steaks and other toothsome dainties on the spot.' In keeping with the British reputation for insatiable tea drinking, the ability to make a brew seems to have been crucial! By 1923 the huts at Felixstowe had been modernised to such an extent that they could offer an electric kettle for the purpose. Unfortunately things have gone backwards since then and very few twenty-first-century huts can boast electricity.

The family posed outside their hut at Tankerton in Kent (see below) probably had to rely on more basic arrangements but they were certainly able to take afternoon tea. A gate-leg table stands ready with its tablecloth; china cups hang from shelves, and taking pride of place on the rear wall is a

This beach hut at Tankerton, Kent, looks like a proper 'home from home', albeit more formal than we are used to today. It has curtains, a table complete with lace cloth and, on the built-in shelves, a teapot and teacups.

By the 1930s beachwear had become considerably less formal. Both the men and women enjoying toffee apples outside this beach hut are wearing shorts.

large teapot. There is a formality about the scene that dates it, yet in two important ways the beach hut was the same then as it is now. It remains a very sociable space, particularly beloved of families; and it looks the same. Unlike other building types, the design has changed surprisingly little over the years.

It was during the inter-war period that beach huts became firmly established. Their number multiplied, formed into rows along and behind the seafront or, at places like Walton-on-the-Naze in Essex, climbing in tiers up the cliff face. Another area of high concentration was the stretch of coast around Bournemouth and Poole. A guidebook of 1941 described the many levels of bungalows covering the cliffs east of Boscombe Pier as 'reminiscent of some Mediterranean hill town'.

Beach huts became so popular during the inter-war period that huge colonies appeared, like this one at Wireless Green, Felixstowe, Suffolk.

Verandas have always been popular with hut owners and there is quite a variety of designs on show in this old view of Walton-on-the-Naze, Essex. Several hundred of differing colours still hug the cliffside today.

Huts built at Herne Bay, Kent, in the 1920s often had an external timber frame to give extra strength as well as decorative interest. The black and white photograph was taken in 1931; the colour image shows some of this type still in use in 2002.

The pretty Suffolk town of Southwold had got its now famous beach huts by 1930. At the end of the decade bathing machines lingered along the seafront, 'though they are no longer hauled in and out with the tide and have practically given place to the more convenient modern bathing-hut and day-bungalow'. It was a similar story elsewhere. Many huts were designed and put up by their owners, a fact recognised by the name of Carpenters' Row at Felixstowe's Brackenbury Fort. Built in their owners' back gardens, they were transported down to the coast a section at a time, all slightly different. Some of the huts at Herne Bay in Kent were built of plywood with an exterior timber frame to give added strength and decorative interest. Bargeboards provided an opportunity for ornamental touches, verandas were popular, and individual tastes also came out in the choice of colour. The basic pattern for beach-hut design was set.

Part of the reason huts grew in popularity was the increased mobility of the population. Since the mid nineteenth century transport routes to the coast had been steadily improving but car ownership permitted a new freedom to come and go. By 1939 there were some three million motor vehicles on the road in Britain, one million of which were private cars. It was becoming easier to get to your beach hut and it no longer had to be close to a railway station. The number of people able to enjoy leisure time was also steadily growing. There

This holiday snap was taken at Frinton-on-Sea, Essex, in August 1925 (note the boy buried up to his neck!). At this date Frinton had two main hut types: those with verandas and those set side-on with small windows in the top corners.

was little time to feel the impact of new legislation before the Second World War but after the war the 1938 Holidays with Pay Act ensured that 80 per cent of the workforce could take time off without losing money.

Measured in visitor numbers, the first two post-war decades represent the true heyday of the British seaside. This was the period of the bucket and spade holiday *par excellence*. Indeed, part of our modern love affair with beach huts is due to the nostalgia they evoke for a time when, we like to think, life was simpler.

The wide sandy beaches of Lincolnshire no longer attract the huge crowds from the Midlands that they did in the 1950s and 1960s but the legacy of past popularity remains in an attractive range of huts. Councils were building huts for hire during the inter-war years and at Sutton-on-Sea the design they chose was particularly appealing. Behind the seawall a platform

These council huts at Sutton-on-Sea, Lincolnshire, have attractive design features including distinctive hipped roofs, window panes in an off-set pattern and balconies with the Art Deco sunburst motif. The interiors were clad in varnished wood.

The pagoda-style hut is unique to Lincolnshire, its roof shape apparently the result of re-using Second World War Nissen huts. The walls are concrete, and behind the shutters are glazed windows and doors.

was created that carried a line of square buildings with hipped roofs, held up on classical columns. Each hut opened on to the promenade but also had windows and doors at the back, where a balcony looking over the putting green was decorated with the quintessential Art Deco motif of a sunburst. The first section of huts was destroyed during the North Sea storm surge of January 1953 but was rebuilt in a simplified version of the same style.

There are similar huts at the neighbouring resort of Mablethorpe, which were joined in the 1950s by flat-roofed blocks and unique pagoda huts. These oriental-looking chalets were made of cast concrete, with their unusual roofs

SOUTH PROMENADE

This 1950s view shows the pagoda huts in use on Mablethorpe's busy South Promenade.

apparently recycled from the inverted sections of wartime Nissen huts. Between Mablethorpe and Skegness (home of the first Butlin's holiday camp, where families slept in chalets the shape and size of beach huts) is Chapel St Leonards. The sands are empty but for a row of private huts, first built in the 1930s by people who used their cars to seek out a quiet place away from habitation.

Around Britain huts remained a popular adjunct to traditional seaside holidays, prompting the continuing renewal of stock. Where the tide left enough exposed sand they were put on the beach, as at Perranporth in

On the same stretch of Lincolnshire coast is Chapel St Leonards. As car ownership became more widespread, this village became a popular place for camping. The quiet beach is overlooked by a row of white huts.

Two families enjoying a happy beach hut holiday in the early Fifties. Huts like this one at Torquay were an important part of the annual seaside holiday.

Swanage beach in the late 1960s. These narrow day huts with white-painted verandas and navy blue bargeboards could be hired from H. Parsons, whose name also appears on the steps going down to the beach.

Because of the large flat beach at Perranporth, the wooden hut blocks were put directly on to the sand. A similar arrangement could be found on Mediterranean beaches and the carefully placed woman in a bikini helps this Cornish scene look warm and enticing.

In the 1960s Ramsgate's St Lawrence Beach got a remarkably modern block of prefabricated concrete beach huts. Two floors were raised above the promenade on pilotis, and alternating colours were used to create architectural rhythm.

In 1958 a three-tiered chalet block was built near Boscombe pier in Dorset. The colourful 'Daleks' on the right were individual changing cubicles for bathers.

Cornwall or Great Yarmouth in Norfolk. More often they were built along concrete promenades at a safe distance from all but the fiercest waves. Some were flat-roofed; others made use of gables to provide shade and decorative character. Among the most overtly modern examples were big multi-level hut blocks whose scale provided greater scope for architectural expression. At Ramsgate's St Lawrence Beach two floors of balconied cubicles rested on slender concrete pilotis. Their design would not have looked out of place at the swiftly expanding foreign resorts of Majorca or the Costa del Sol. The Overstrand Building, which opened at Boscombe in 1958, was another big statement of faith in domestic tourism. With its curved and receding ends, it had a more nautical feel, enhanced by the motifs of fishes and boats decorating the balcony railings.

The balconies at Boscombe, which are decorated with stylised fish and sailing boats, before restoration as part of a major regeneration project.

Yet at the same time the long-established habit of visiting the British coast was beginning to be challenged by the new possibilities of travel abroad. Beach huts were ideal for when it rained, but how much better would it be if you could go somewhere where you knew that it would not rain? By the end of the twentieth century some places had lost their huts altogether and the presence of shabby, under-occupied blocks contributed to a depressing sense of doom at the seaside.

As the next chapter will show, that has changed. For proof we need look only as far as Boscombe's Overstrand Building, now transformed into 'super chalets' and 'surf pods' by designers Wayne and Geraldine Hemingway, ready to welcome visitors to the United Kingdom's first artificial surf reef.

BEACH HUTS: PRESENT AND FUTURE

SINCE the late 1990s, beach huts have experienced a dramatic change of image. Although they have been popular since their introduction, huts have not always been fashionable. Now they are – perhaps more so than at any other point in their history. Their appeal reached its lowest point during the last quarter of the twentieth century. Then, in the late 1990s, stories began to appear in the press about rising prices at smart places such as Southwold and Mudeford. This phenomenon was not based on reinventing the beach hut; indeed the opposite was true. Neither the look nor the function of beach huts had changed at all. The shift was one of perception. In a period of rapid technological advance the rediscovery of simple seaside pleasures was symbolised by a refreshingly low-tech structure. The lack of electricity and water supply, the small size and the general ban on overnight stays would be drawbacks anywhere else; as far as beach huts are concerned, getting back to basics is part of the attraction.

A blackboard advertising beach huts for hire at Saunton, on the north Devon coast.

Despite the increased prominence of beach huts in the media, the number available around the British coast remains surprisingly low. In the absence of official statistics some estimates have suggested there may be as many as three-quarters of a million but the figure for England and Wales is actually closer to 25,000, with the highest concentrations on the south and east coasts. Some small clusters can also be found in Scotland. Most are on public beaches, owned and managed by local authorities, but private beaches have huts too, for both short- and long-term hire. The number at any location can range from between ten and twenty, up to a thousand or more; very rarely does supply meet demand.

Journalists documenting the beach-hut boom have focused their attention on a few places that have become famous as a result. The 245 pretty huts at Southwold were noted by guidebook writers from the 1930s onwards but they rarely appeared in photographs or postcard views of the sedate Suffolk town. Then suddenly, in the mid 1990s, they were everywhere, appearing in films, on television and in national newspapers. Southwold's old-fashioned charm had struck a chord and demand for its huts, each measuring just 80

Opposite: Under the cliff at Newquay's Tolcarne Beach there are four terraces of small white huts. With their doors painted sun-bleached shades of blue, red, yellow and green, these Cornish huts would look at home on a Greek island.

Some of Britain's most sought-after huts are at Southwold in Suffolk. These ones below Gun Hill command the highest prices. The front verandas are a typical feature of all huts along the promenade.

The colourful huts on West Beach at Whitstable in Kent are easily accessible from London; the railway line runs directly behind them. Tracey Emin's hut stood here until it was turned into a work of art.

square feet, soared. In 1995 huts in the best area, Gun Hill, could be had for about £12,000, a figure that was already considered expensive. Five years later they had more than doubled in value and a Southwold beach hut could cost more than a two-bedroom terraced house in nearby Lowestoft.

Such inflated values reflect the importance of location. The land on which the huts sit is only leased; it belongs to the local council, whose annual rates have to be paid in addition to the purchase price. But, because the number of huts available is strictly limited, there are people willing to pay as much as necessary. Like using an early bathing machine, owning a beach hut at Southwold has become a status symbol.

At Whitstable, on the north Kent coast, the annual Oyster Festival and the town's proximity to London have ensured a new trendiness, in which the beach huts play a key part, though their prices have not risen to the same extent as at Southwold. The most famous Whitstable hut was the one taken away from the beach by the artist Tracey Emin. She turned her former weekend retreat into a work of art entitled *The Last Thing I Said Was Don't Leave Me*. It was acquired in 1999 for £75,000 for Charles Saatchi's collection and was exhibited in New York. Emin's blue hut was deliberately ramshackle but those left behind on the West Beach have been smartened up, often featuring in interior design magazines. The slopes at Tankerton, on the eastern fringe of Whitstable, are also enjoying a new hut heyday.

Yet the most staggering evidence of the beach-hut boom has been on a strip of sand in Dorset, where two lines of colourful wooden structures curve back to back along the spine of Mudeford Sandbank, one row looking across a large natural harbour toward Christchurch, the other facing seaward. Not only do these 354 huts enjoy a unique location but their owners are also permitted to live in them for up to nine months of the year. In terms of size and services they are basic: approximately 12 feet square, with no mains water, electricity or drainage. Since 1968 cars have been banned and the only way to get on to the sand spit is by boat or on the miniature train across Hengistbury Head. Far from being a disadvantage, this relative isolation is treasured by residents and coveted by visitors, so much so that the huts, which used to provide a cheap family holiday, are now worth a fortune. As Tim Baber, a long-time resident and editor of the *Mudeford Sandbank News*, has put it: 'you've either got to be lucky or rich to have one.'

Luck, in the case of beach huts, usually means inheritance. It is quite common for a hut to be handed through the generations, which explains

The 354 huts on Mudeford Sandbank, Dorset, enjoy an idyllic location. Overnight stays are permitted for nine months of the year, so owners can wake up to views of the Isle of Wight or Christchurch harbour, depending on which way their beach hut faces.

Above:
Heather and Tony Payne outside 'Gulls and Buoys' in August 2002. The hut at Lyme Regis in Dorset was built for Heather's father in 1952.

Above right:
Olive Pigney in her hut at Wells-next-the-Sea, Norfolk. When she bought 'Prongs' in 1984, it was already sixty years old (see page 36). Olive's family have always had beach huts at Wells and she remembers the first one erected by her grandfather in 1919. Before that the family had a beach tent.

why, at some places, they rarely come on the market. Families who held on to their unfashionable huts through the 1970s and 1980s are now in an enviable position. Some have decided to cash in but others vow they never will. A hut inherited from parents or grandparents can mean more to some people than the house where they live – it has usually been a part of their life for longer. Even the seasonal leases for council huts have traditionally rolled on year after year so there can be fierce competition when one becomes available. Waiting lists can be as long as ten years.

Whatever an owner's tastes, practical considerations of upkeep and security have an impact on beach-hut design. Most detached huts are built of wood and must be regularly coated with paint or stain to ensure they stay weather- and water-proof. Other materials have been tested, including fibreglass, unplasticised polyvinyl chloride (UPVC) and latterly glass reinforced plastic (GRP), but none of these can rival the natural appeal of timber.

Owing to the changeable and often fierce seaside weather, huts on the promenade or at the top of the beach sometimes have to be tied down. Others are built on stilts to protect them from high tides. Raising any hut even slightly off the beach helps to keep the floor dry and well ventilated, making it less susceptible to rot. Two contrasting examples of huts on stilts can be seen at Wells-next-the-Sea in Norfolk and Frinton-on-Sea in Essex.

The first presents a jolly row of colourful cabins, the second a sturdy and more sombre parade of huts that are completely suspended above the waves at high tide.

Out of season many huts go into hibernation. In autumn a crane lifts the huts north of Southwold Pier into a car park behind the seawall. At Whitby

Above: Most huts at Wells-next-the-Sea in Norfolk are on stilts. Older huts tend to be a simple box design but newer ones, like those in the foreground, typically have verandas and front decks.

Left: The Whalings at Frinton-on-Sea, Essex. At the front these huts are level with the promenade but on the seaward side they rest on a timber platform with concrete pilings. Although there is no direct beach access, owners can hear the sea below them at high tide.

Above:
Free-standing huts are sometimes secured to the seawall, though this one trussed up at Bexhill-on-Sea, Sussex, is quite an extreme case.

Above right:
At Littlehampton in Sussex huts are arranged in crescents behind the beach. The half-height shutters deter vandals and fold down into a useful sun deck.

in Yorkshire huts are stored in the shaft of the West Cliff lift, where repairs and repainting can be done ready for the following summer. Other huts are moved into barns or fields, while some private huts temporarily revert to being garden sheds.

Aside from natural threats, beach huts are also the unfortunate prey of vandals. In the 1950s the majority had glazing but windows have become increasingly less common. Sometimes the glass is merely hidden behind heavy shutters that can be turned into useful or decorative features. At places such as Littlehampton in Sussex and Lyme Regis in Dorset shutters are hinged at the bottom so that they can fold down into a handy area of outside decking. Where there is no colour restriction on huts, the shutters are occasionally covered with attractive murals.

Almost every hut location comes with some form of constraint from the landowner. With day huts, the principal limitation applies to occupancy and usually excludes overnight stays. Hut size is also generally regulated for the sake of consistency, whereas the dictates on decoration vary widely. Colour schemes can be rigidly enforced or a marvellous free-for-all. Along the stretch of Sussex shoreline managed by Worthing Borough Council all huts have to be white. Elsewhere monotone walls are enlivened by coloured

All the huts at Hove in Sussex have green tops and burgundy bottoms. The choice of door colour is left to individual owners.

doors. There are many examples of this in the West Country: at Paignton and Torquay the white gabled huts sport a diverse range of door shades; under flat roofs, the doors at Woolacombe are brightly consecutive in red, yellow, green and blue. Below the Cornish cliffs of Newquay's Tolcarne Beach the same colours appear in sun-bleached tones, each on a different level: green

The colours of this painstakingly striped hut, called 'Upper Deck', at Tankerton in Kent evoke other seaside structures such as lighthouses or Punch and Judy tents.

Beach-hut names provide an opportunity for decoration as well as creative thinking. These examples all come from Southwold in Suffolk, where almost every hut has a name.

above yellow, above red, above blue. These popular colours are also consecutively applied to entire huts at Whitby and on the National Trust's beach at Llanbedrog in Gwynedd, Wales. At Hove, in Sussex, the highly distinctive huts all have the same pale green top halves and burgundy bottoms but every door is a different colour of the rainbow.

The beach is a good source for interior design accessories. Driftwood and shells are often used by owners like Pat Allen, from Folkestone in Kent, whose hut interior has an appropriately nautical theme.

Perhaps significantly, the most sought-after beaches, including Mudeford Sandbank, Southwold, Whitstable and Wells-next-the-Sea, have no restraints on colour. Owners are allowed creative freedom to express themselves, something that can also be seen in the choice of hut names. Many follow a maritime theme inspired by the beach, the sea, birds, fish and shells.

New hut blocks were built at Lowestoft in Suffolk during the late 1990s. Above the colourful stable doors are small triangular windows designed to be out of vandals' reach.

Brand-new huts at Scarborough's North Bay. The extending gables are held up on chunky stepped brackets, which look particularly effective receding into the distance.

Some playfully highlight the hut as an escape, for example 'Lazy Days', 'Forty Winks' or 'Paradise Found'. Others are the result of family mythologies inexplicable to the casual passer-by.

Given external constraints, it is often the interior that gets the most personal decorative treatment. Despite the inherent vulnerability of beach

The pastel-painted beach huts at St George's Road, Southsea, Hampshire, use the traditional gabled shape but are unusually tall.

huts, the new breed of owner is often willing to spend a lot of money on furnishings, seeing their seaside getaway as an extension of home. This trend has undoubtedly been encouraged by journalists, as well as by programmes such as the BBC's *Changing Rooms*, which created two designer beach huts. Things have changed since the days when beach-hut interiors were more likely to be filled with a random selection of cast-off furniture and crockery. Flotsam and jetsam have always made great accessories but nowadays there is also a growing commercial market in seaside-themed items. The beach-hut image is so popular that it can be found on items from mugs to bath mats, key-rings to cushions – everything that is necessary to kit out a one-room retreat.

With this increased design sensitivity among hut owners, it may seem surprising that the basic architectural form remains so essentially similar to the bathing machine. In the twenty-first century new brick blocks have been built at Lowestoft and Bridlington. Dawlish Warren, Southsea, Seaford and Scarborough's North Bay all have brightly coloured new huts, yet all offer a variation on the same theme of a gabled cabin. It may be that this is exactly what people want from their beach huts, but an international architectural competition, part-funded by the European Regional Development Fund, Lincolnshire County Council and East Lindsey District Council, points the way to an even more exciting future for the humble hut. Bathing Beauties™, the brainchild of artist Michael Trainor, is a project that has helped refocus interest on the open skies and golden sands of Lincolnshire. More than 240

Below left: 'Come Up and See Me' is one of the Bathing Beauties™ available to hire from East Lindsey District Council. Designed by Michael Trainor and built along the South Promenade at Mablethorpe in Lincolnshire, this beach hut resembles a giant gin and tonic made of vitrified tiles, mirror, laminated plywood and galvanised steel.

Below: 'Jabba' was designed as a contemporary cave by I-am Associates Ltd, London. A winner in the Bathing Beauties™ competition, it has been built in the sand dunes at Mablethorpe in Lincolnshire.

Looking out to sea from 'Halcyon Hut', a winning entry in the Bathing Beauties™ competition, designed by Canadian architects Atelier NU. The walls are built of thin planks of cedar interspersed with clear acrylic to let the light in.

designers from fifteen countries sent scale models of their twenty-first-century beach huts to Mablethorpe for judging in 2006. The creative range of entries was phenomenal, a true challenge to the 'traditional' hut, and some of the winning designs have actually been built. As part of a linear gallery of seaside architecture, these quirky structures, including 'Come Up and See Me', based on a giant gin and tonic, and the contemporary cave that is 'Jabba', are now available to hire from the local council.

Enjoying huge public popularity, and with such convincing proof of their potential for reinvention, beach huts look set to remain our favourite seaside structures for many years to come.

FURTHER READING

Anderson, Janice, and Swinglehurst, Edmund. *The Victorian and Edwardian Seaside*. Bounty Books, second edition 2005.

Bathing Beauties: Re-imagining the Beach Hut for the Twenty-first Century. Exhibition catalogue. Hub: The National Centre for Craft and Design, 2007.

Berry, Sue. *Georgian Brighton*. Phillimore & Co, 2005.

Braggs, Steven, and Harris, Diane. *Sun, Fun and Crowds: Seaside Holidays between the Wars*. Tempus Publishing, 2000.

Brodie, Allan, and Winter, Gary. *England's Seaside Resorts*. English Heritage, 2007.

Ferry, Kathryn. *Sheds on the Seashore: A tour through beach hut history.* Indepen Press, 2009.

Gray, Fred. *Designing the Seaside: Architecture, Society and Nature*. Reaktion, 2006.

Green, Rod. *Beach Huts*. Cassell Illustrated, 2005.

Hannavy, John. *The English Seaside in Victorian and Edwardian Times*. Shire, 2003.

Howell, Sarah. *The Seaside*. Studio Vista, 1974.

King, Anthony D. *The Bungalow: The Production of a Global Culture*. Oxford University Press, 1995.

Lansdell, Avril. *Seaside Fashions 1860–1939: A Study of Clothes Worn in or beside the Sea*. Shire, 1990.

Lenček, Lena, and Bosker, Gideon. *The Beach: The History of Paradise on Earth*. Pimlico, 1999.

Lindley, Kenneth. *Seaside Architecture*. Hugh Evelyn, 1973.

Marsden, Christopher. *The English at the Seaside*. Collins, 1957.

Pearson, Lynn F. *Piers and Other Seaside Architecture*. Shire, 2002.

Walton, John K. *The English Seaside Resort: A Social History, 1870–1914*. Leicester University Press, 1983.

Walton, John K. *The British Seaside: Holidays and Resorts in the Twentieth Century*. Manchester University Press, 2000.

GAZETTEER

Although there are beach huts in Scotland and Wales, the majority can be found around the English coast. The numbers at each place vary but all the places listed below have day huts.

CORNWALL
Bude, Falmouth (Swanpool Beach), Newquay, Par, St Ives, Widemouth Bay.

DEVON
Beer, Budleigh Salterton, Dawlish, Dawlish Warren, Exmouth, Paignton, Plymouth, Saunton Sands, Seaton, Sidmouth, Teignmouth, Torquay, Westward Ho!, Woolacombe.

DORSET
Bournemouth, Boscombe, Charmouth, Christchurch (Friars Cliff), Hamworthy, Lyme Regis, Mudeford (Avon Beach), Mudeford Sandbank, Poole, Portland Bill, Sandbanks, Southbourne, Studland Bay, Swanage, Weymouth.

ESSEX
Brightlingsea, Clacton-on-Sea, Dovercourt, Frinton-on-Sea, Harwich, Holland-on-Sea, Shoeburyness, Southend-on-Sea, Walton-on-the-Naze, Westcliff, West Mersea.

HAMPSHIRE
Barton-on-Sea, Calshot Spit, Fareham, Gosport (Stokes Bay), Hayling Island, Hordle Cliff, Lee-on-the-Solent, Milford-on-Sea, Southsea.

ISLE OF WIGHT
Bembridge, Colwell Bay, Forelands, Gurnard, Lake, St Helens, Sandown, Seaview (Puckpool Park), Shanklin, Small Hope, Totland Bay, Ventnor.

KENT
Birchington, Broadstairs, Folkestone, Herne Bay, Hythe, Kingsdown, Kingsgate Bay, Margate (Westbrook Bay), Romney Marsh, St Margaret's Bay, Seasalter, Tankerton, Whitstable.

LANCASHIRE
Fleetwood.

LINCOLNSHIRE
Chapel St Leonards, Cleethorpes, Mablethorpe, Sandilands, Skegness, Sutton-on-Sea.

NORFOLK
Brancaster, Cromer, Gorleston, Great Yarmouth, Heacham, Hunstanton (Old and New), Mundesley, Sheringham, Wells-next-the-Sea.

SUFFOLK
Felixstowe, Lowestoft, Pakefield, Sizewell, Southwold, Walberswick.

SUSSEX
Angmering, Bexhill, Bognor Regis (Aldwick Beach), Brighton (Madeira Drive), Cooden, East Wittering, Eastbourne, Felpham, Ferring, Goring-by-Sea, Hove, Lancing, Littlehampton, Ovingdean, Rottingdean, Rustington, St Leonards-on-Sea (West of Haven), Saltdean, Seaford, Shoreham, West Wittering, Worthing.

YORKSHIRE
Bridlington, Filey, Hornsea, Saltburn-by-the-Sea, Scarborough, Whitby.

SCOTLAND
Coldingham Bay (Berwickshire), Hopeman Bay (Moray Firth).

WALES
Abersoch (Gwynedd), Llanbedrog (Gwynedd), Langland Bay (Swansea).

Bathing machines

A small number of bathing machines have survived. These can be seen at the following places:

Weymouth Timewalk Museum, Brewer's Quay, Hope Square, Weymouth, Dorset DT4 8TR. Telephone: 01305 777622.
   Website: www.weymouth.gov.uk
Langham Hotel, Royal Parade, Eastbourne, Sussex BN22 7AH.
   Telephone: 01323 731451. Website: www.langhamhotel.co.uk
Seaford Museum, Martello Tower, Esplanade, Seaford, East Sussex BN25 9BH. Telephone: 01323 898222. Website: www.seafordmuseum.co.uk

INDEX

Page numbers in italic refer to illustrations